POLAR BABIES

CARIBOU CALVES

by Genevieve Nilsen

TABLE OF CONTENTS

tadpole books

WORDS TO KNOW

antlers

calf

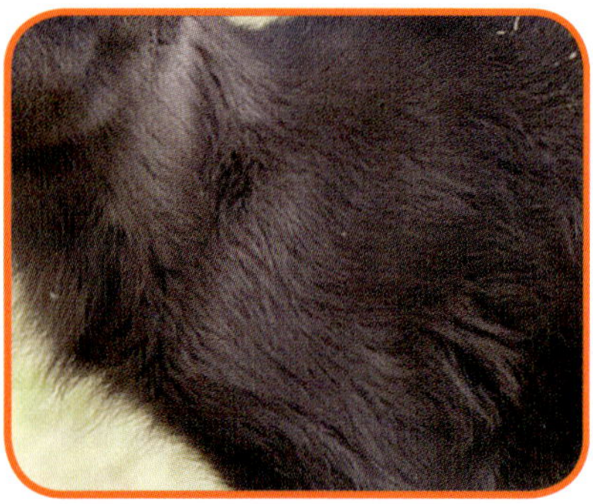

fur

group

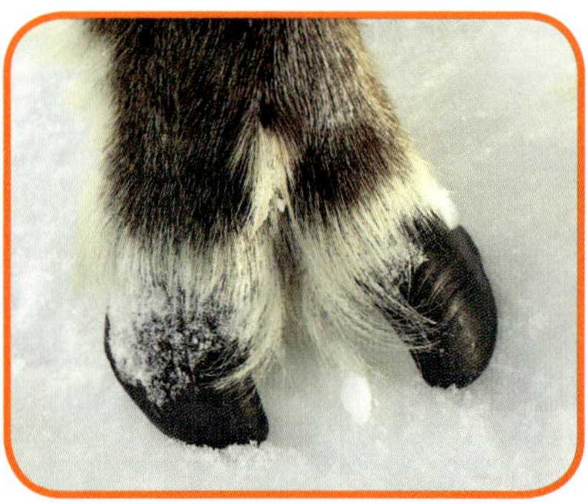

hooves

snow

CARIBOU CALVES

This caribou calf is new.

It stands right away.

It is in a group.

It walks far.

It has hooves.

It walks on snow.

It has fur.

It is dark.

It stays warm.

It grows big.

It grows antlers!

LET'S REVIEW!

What does a caribou have that helps it walk and stay warm in snow?

INDEX